D0707535

OVERCOMING SIN & ENJOYING GOD

by Danny Bond

THE WORD FOR TODAY

P.O. Box 8000, Costa Mesa, CA 92628

Overcoming Sin and Enjoying God
by Danny Bond
General Editor: Chuck Smith

Published by **The Word For Today**
P.O. Box 8000, Costa Mesa, CA 92628

© 1996 The Word For Today

ISBN 0–936728–69-8

All Rights Reserved. No part of this publication may be reproduced, stored in a retrieval system, or transmitted in any form or by any means without the express written consent of **The Word For Today Publishers.**

Unless otherwise indicated, Scripture quotations in this book are taken from the New King James Version of the Bible. Copyright © 1979, 1980, 1982 by Thomas Nelson, Inc., Publisher. Used by permission.

TABLE OF CONTENTS

Preface

When Luke wrote the message of the gospel to Theophilus, he declared that his desire was to set forth in order a declaration of those things that are most surely believed among us. Luke desired that Theophilus might know the certainty of those things in which he had been instructed.

We seem to be living in a day of spiritual confusion. Paul wrote to the Ephesians that they not be as children, tossed to and fro with every wind of doctrine by the slight of men and the cunning craftiness whereby they lie in wait to deceive. Because of all the confusion in the church today, and the many winds of doctrine that continue to blow through the body of Christ, we felt that it would be good to have various pastors write booklets that would address the issues and give to you the solid biblical basis of what we believe and why we believe it.

Our purpose is that the spiritual house that you build will be set upon the solid foundation of the eternal Word of God, thus we know that it can withstand the fiercest storms.

Pastor Chuck Smith
Calvary Chapel of Costa Mesa, California

INTRODUCTION

God is in the business of making bad people good. Even Charles Darwin, the man who contributed so much to evolutionary thinking, admitted this. He once wrote to a minister: "Your services have done more for our village in a few months than all our efforts for many years. We have never been able to reclaim a single drunkard, but through your services I do not know that there is a drunkard left in the village!" Later Darwin visited the island of Tierra del Fuego at the southern tip of South America. What he found among the people was horrifying—savagery and bestiality almost beyond description. But when he returned after a missionary had worked among the people, he was amazed at the change in them. He acknowledged that the Gospel does transform lives. In fact, he was so moved by what he saw that he contributed money to the mission until his death.

Truly going from bad to good in life can only be accomplished through Jesus Christ. Yet it seems that so much misunderstanding exists about battling sin while enjoying our relationship with God. Even if you have walked with the Lord for decades, you will still battle with your sin. It's a constant fight. Sometimes you may fall and don't understand how to gain victory. That can cause pain that is needlessly carried for years. "How do I achieve victory? What if I blow it and make God mad at me? How do I get off this chaotic yo–yo Christian experience I'm living and become stable?" All valid questions you might have asked. They will be answered. And that is a primary reason for writing this book—to help ease your pain and raise your level of joy!

CHAPTER 1
THE ONE TIME GIFT OF JUSTIFICATION

Nobody has understood Christianity who does not understand. . . the word "justified."
—John R. W. Stott

There is a sense in which Mr. Stott's words are the perfect words to begin this book. If I set off into my Christian life unclear on justification, I will leave myself open to endless deceptions from Satan, and as a result I will be joyless far too often. It would be impossible to overstate the importance of this issue. This is the foundation upon which everything else must be built. Before we can make any effort to overcome sin, we must be able to rest in this completely. Then we can carry that rest with us into the battles ahead. Don't miss this great truth. Let it sink deep into your heart over the next few pages.

The Ultimate Declaration

Justification is an act of God, whereby He declares you righteous in His sight. This declaration is so vast and sweeping, that its effect is to bring total forgiveness for all sin—past, present and future. To put it in Biblical terms, God has separated our transgressions from us as far as the east is from the west (Psalm 103:12). This is an unmerited gift, granted to you solely by His grace through faith in Jesus Christ. You might ask, "But I thought I was supposed to keep God's law and do good works, so He can save me?" No! You must understand that the entire plan of redemption was set in place in eternity past, because man's most righteous works are filthy rags in the eyes of our Holy God (Isaiah 64:6). How good it is to read in God's Word that we are freely justified by His grace through the redemption that came by Jesus Christ (Romans 3:24).

The Ultimate Satisfaction

If there be ground for you to trust in your own righteousness, then all that Christ did to purchase salvation, and all that God did to prepare the way for it, is in vain.

—Jonathan Edwards

One of the greatest contributing factors to my peace and joy as a Christian, is the reality that God accepts me, in spite of the fact I still struggle with sin and disobedience. Here is the reason why: Jesus Christ hides our unrighteousness with His righteousness. At the same time, He covers our disobedience with His obedience, and He shadows our death with His death, that the judgment of God cannot find us. Without question this is one of the most liberating truths in all of the Bible.

> *But to him who does not work but believes on Him who justifies the ungodly, his faith is accounted for righteousness.*
> —Romans 4:5

Have you ever come back to God after a really bad month, vowing to do better because you feel that your salvation is in jeopardy? Perhaps you have thought that God is angry with you and He wants you perform a chain of good works to calm Him down? That somehow this will cause Him to once again "accept you" and bless you? Do you add to that repeated pleas for forgiveness, hoping that maybe after the fifth or sixth time He will give in and bless you? If you have been living like that, it is because of a lack of understanding of justification.

Being clothed in the righteousness of Christ, you are accepted as if you had never sinned. Actually it is even beyond that. Even if you had never sinned, you could only have stood in the righteousness of man. But now by faith in Jesus Christ, you stand in the righteousness of God Himself! In terms of your *position* before God, you are as righteous as you can ever possibly be. In terms of your *practice*, you will continue to fight against sin in your body, but that is what sanctification is all about. Let's settle it right here. It is your position in Christ that gives you complete acceptance before God, not your daily performance.

I have come to really treasure this truth; that from the moment I became God's child, He has related to me as a fully justified sinner, and never again as a wretched one.

> *Let us therefore come boldly to the throne of grace, that we may obtain mercy and find grace to help in time of need.*
>
> —Hebrews 4:16

I no longer come in a season of failure nervously offering some good work to try to earn His favor. I come gratefully anticipating His mercy and grace.

The Ultimate Protection

Justification takes place in the mind of God and not in the nervous system of the believer.
—C. I. Scofield

As I face the battles with sin and Satan in my life, the doctrine of justification becomes a great source of protection. The Bible tells us the devil is the accuser of God's people (Revelation 12:10). He tempts you into sin and then condemns you afterward, leaving you feeling miserable and afraid to go back into fellowship with God. His goal is to alienate you from God through discouragement.

The story is told of how the devil once advertised his tools for sale at a public auction. When the prospective buyers assembled, there was one oddly shaped tool which was labeled "not for sale." Asked to explain why this was, the devil answered, "I can spare my other tools, but I cannot spare this one. It is the most useful implement I have. It is called Discouragement, and with it I can work my way into hearts otherwise inaccessible."

How many times has Satan paralyzed you with discouragement after you have experienced failure with some sin? Paul tells us in Ephesians

6:14, that we can stand against the devil in victory if we have on the "breastplate of righteousness." Have you ever wondered how you put on this breastplate? You put it on by applying yourself to a clear understanding of justification by faith. By declaring you righteous, God has also declared His great love for you. He is for you. He will lead you through all your victories, and comfort you in every defeat. Knowing these things, we take our position in the battle with our confidence placed in God.

> *What then shall we say to these things? If God is for us, who can be against us? He who did not spare His own Son, but delivered Him up for us all, how shall He not with Him also freely give us all things? Who shall bring a charge against God's elect? It is God who justifies. Who is he who condemns? It is Christ who died, and furthermore is also risen, who is even at the right hand of God, who also makes intercession for us.*
>
> —Romans 8:31-34

So begin your life of overcoming sin while enjoying God with this great truth, and it will serve you well. In so many ways, this will be the truth that will make you free in all your future battles.

CHAPTER 2
THE LIFETIME PROCESS OF SANCTIFICATION

A second basic principle that requires clear understanding is **sanctification**. This God–ordained process provides the born again believer the ability to daily deal with sin and continue to enjoy God. What is sanctification? It means being separated unto God and living an upright, holy life before Him. It signifies a coming out from among the ways of the world and being separate in your life to God.

Sanctification begins at the moment you are justified by God. It, however, is not a once for all act like justification. We all come from different places and have different sins, hang–ups and problems. That's part of our unique character as sinners. God moves each of us toward one individual and His likeness, Jesus Christ. So, the end of your sanctification is a Christ–like life. It is our cooperation with His power that really makes up sanctification. Sanctification is all about being set apart to God to know Him and to enjoy Him, being free from the entanglements of this world.

In terms of every day living, it is a lifelong process from here to there. At the moment of justification, you are given a position before God that is perfect, flawless and permanent based on Christ's sacrifice on the cross. In a practical sense, you will slowly begin to change and begin to catch up with your positional standing. When you die, He glorifies you with the glory of Christ. Then you eternally have the fullness of His image.

In the meantime, the Holy Spirit works this process in your life on His time clock. That means that He has His own list of priorities for your life. Are you ever in a hurry? Do you wish you could be holy all at once? What was one of your biggest problems that you asked deliverance from when Christ came into your heart? Many years ago at my conversion, my biggest request was to get off drugs and alcohol.

I didn't want a 12–step program; I wanted it done instantly, and God granted my prayer. God in His sovereignty may take more time for others. For every believer, though, it is only the beginning of His work in each of our lives. This is what sanctification is all about.

It has been well said that the pathway to holiness is paved with a sense of your own wretchedness. The holier you get, the more you hate your own sin. A great tension exists throughout the life of every believer. You hate your own sin and, simultaneously, with greater understanding, you grow closer to Jesus. With increasing understanding, you rest more deeply in His grace as the years go by.

I'm sure you can recall at the beginning of your Christian walk, those times when you were suddenly delivered. The Holy Spirit has His priority list for your life and you have yours. Some of those items have been crossed off your list. That's because He has worked there. Other things you keep bringing to Him and you wait. Be patient and allow Him to work in His time.

It is analogous to a mall or a department store. They are always under construction, constantly changing their look so you will feel like you are in a new place and want to come back. They have signs that say, "Pardon our dust—Under Construction," and they invite you to come in. As Christians, we are always under construction. Dust is always flying because God is always working. Learn to be happy and continue to know and walk with Him in the midst of the dust. You are constantly covered by grace while the dust is still flying. You began your Christian walk by His grace and it will end by His grace.

So, as you seek to mortify the sin in your life, you'll have some really good times and also some pretty bad experiences. Understand though, that through it all you are covered by grace. When you fall in your worst hour, you learn that you fall into grace. God the Father, through Christ, has done the most important work. He made you fit for Heaven. Now the Holy Spirit, on His time clock and with His priority list, is changing your life practically, bit by bit, so you can enjoy God in an experiential way.

Walking Through Your Promised Land

The Children of Israel illustrate the sanctification process in every Christian. When they entered that wonderful land of promise, did they conquer it all at once? No. Could they enjoy what they had conquered? Yes. Why? Because as they moved through the Promised Land, they conquered it in God's power. That's the key. When God wanted a battle won, He demonstrated His power. Once He sent a bunch of bees and another time He parted the Red Sea. He even caused the enemies of God's people to fight and kill themselves instead of having the soldiers of Israel go into combat. He continually did unusual things; yet, it was always His power that controlled the situation. As long as He led and empowered them, His people conquered and enjoyed the land that was taken. When they did not seek God's leading, however, they suffered defeat. This is a principle to follow. It is the same in living the Christian life today.

When Joshua first led the people into the Promised Land, he was visited by men wearing old clothes and carrying moldy bread. They said they had come from a great distance and told Joshua they wanted to make a covenant, be friends and work together. What did Joshua do? He looked at them and believed their story. But he didn't seek the Lord's counsel and failed to ask for His guidance and direction. Had he done that, he would have discovered that these "friends" were Gibeonites trying to deceive him and his people. They succeeded and the sin of the Gibeonites infiltrated the Israelites. Ultimately, because they didn't let God lead them, the Israelites sinned just like the Gibeonites.

Sanctification is much like that. You need to come to that place in your life where you thank God and enjoy the land He has already given you. Force yourself, if need be, to focus on what He has done, not on what He hasn't done.

Something once said by a one–time wicked and immoral slave trader illustrates well this point. **"I am not what I hope to be; I am not what I even should be; but praise God, I am not what I was."** God captured this man's heart and converted him. Toward the end of his life, John Newton became a great and wonderful pastor. He wrote the hymn, "Amazing Grace," and coined that phrase which has ministered to me for years. If you are only concerned about what God has not done in your life, remember this: **you also are not what you once were!** If you are His child, you are changed! He is working in your life and has already done more than you expected or deserve.

Eclipsing the Good With the Bad

Perhaps this analogy will cause this truth to stick with you. Have you ever taken a coin and held it up to one eye and closed the other eye to block out the sun? As big as it is, the sun is completely blotted out by a very small coin! Here's the point: You can become so focused on specific areas of your life, that you can't see anything else. Certainly there are issues in which God has not yet worked, but He will. Wait patiently for Him.

Which person are you? The one who holds the coin far away from your face, exposing all the light and beauty there is to see, or are you the one who holds it directly up to your eye blocking your view of all that He has done and is doing? God wants us all to have the proper perspective.

CHAPTER 3
LAYING HOLD OF WHAT IS OURS

The Lord Gives Us a Condition

Now let's take a close look at Romans 8:13 which tell us,

> *For if you live according to the flesh you will die; but if by the Spirit you put to death the deeds of the body, you will live.*

Notice there is a condition here. Paul shows it to us in verse 13, **"but if."** He explains that those who are actively involved in putting sin to death in their lives, by the power of the Spirit, enjoy the fullness of this life.

You might say, "But I'm not able to do that!" You're right! You can't do it by yourself. He says, *"if by the Spirit you put to death the deeds of the body, you will live."* God is saying, "Look, I've given you the power to do it in the Spirit. Depend on Me to empower you. If you will do this, I will fulfill My promise to you." It is a certainty because it's His promise!

You cannot out give God. The more you give to Him, the more He gives back to you. Any blessing that you lay hold of as yours, is a gift to you by the grace of God. You can't earn it. Any blessing you enjoy, comes to you because of your standing in grace, and that has come to you solely by the blood of Jesus through the grace of God. Everything in the entire Christian life that is yours, that you will experience now and in the future, is His gift of grace. You do not earn blessings in the Christian life, you apprehend them. So, the idea in this verse is that you overcome the sin that stands between you and the blessing.

If, for example, you are living in some great sin and try to read your Bible, you will think the Bible is dry. Why is it dry? Between you and the blessing is that sin. Instead, you must maneuver yourself underneath the spout where the glory comes out—to get underneath the blessing.

I remember a time when I was hiking a

remote trail in Hawaii. The farther I went the
thirstier I got. I was totally unprepared, had no
water, and was about to collapse. So, I turned
around and headed back to where I started.
Shortly, another hiker approached me with a
water container, handed it to me and I drank
and drank. I remember him telling me about a
waterfall not far off the path I was hiking. He
explained how to get there and assured me that,
if I stood under that waterfall, I would have all
the refreshment I could ever want. But I had to
go down that path and **follow the directions** he
gave to reach the waterfall. Otherwise, I would
never get there. Well, I followed his directions
and found the waterfall. Standing under that
falling water was one of the most incredible
experiences of my life.

You must maneuver your way to where the
blessedness exists for you in the Christian life,
and overcome the sin that would block your
way. You are not earning the blessings; you are
apprehending them, laying hold of them. Paul,
in Philippians, calls this the *"upward call of God in
Christ."*

This isn't legalism. It's fighting your way
into full light. There is a major difference

between the two. You begin to realize that the holy life is the happy life, and you do what is necessary to apprehend and enjoy it.

The Lord Gives Us the Power

This is the same result he talks about in Galatians 6:8, *"If you sow to the Spirit, you will reap everlasting life."* This isn't so much being born again as it is experiencing abundant life. This is the life of God permeating the soul of man. That's the experience. It's the idea of rivers of living water, or the overflowing cup that David declares in Psalm 23. It is the peace that passes understanding, and it is enjoying intimacy with God. It allows you to look people squarely in the eye with a clean conscience. You get all of this, if you, **by the Spirit**, put to death the deeds of the body. You will live in all these dimensions as a Christian. Lay hold of all that God has for you.

The power is God's. Do you remember trying to change before you were a Christian? Did you ever vow to change? Did you ever make a New Year's resolution? Have you ever kept one? You vowed to change but couldn't because you didn't have the power to change. That power comes only from God to do for you what you can never do for yourself. He's committed to finish what He has begun, and that's where you rest. That is where your dependency lies.

I thank God that, though I am not perfect, I am saved by His grace. So it is with you. When I am excelling and advancing and conquering sin, it's because of His grace and His Spirit. The same is true for you. When I trip and fall, He picks me up and moves me on again, because of His grace and the work of His Holy Spirit within me. It is just as true for you, too.

Thank God for what He has done for you. Let God work and let Him love you. Allow Him to show you how strong He is in your weakness and on your behalf. Be patient. In so doing, you will *"possess your soul,"* as the Bible says, and enjoy your great and gracious God. He has loved you enough to save you and is committed to finish in you what He has begun.

God is in the business of making bad people good. He takes people bound in sin and sets them free. God does this because He created man for fellowship with Himself. The highest level of enjoyment of God is experienced when man is free from a preoccupation with sin in his own life. Gaze upon, adore and interact with the Lord. This is the first step in finding completeness and being able to walk in freedom from sin.

CHAPTER 4

AVOIDING WHAT DOESN'T WORK

A Sinless Perfection?

Let's continue to dispel any confusion about this important issue by examining five approaches that have classically been misleading and ineffective. First, Paul is not talking about **a sinless perfection** when he states, *"if by the Spirit you put to death the deeds [or misdeeds] of the body, you will live."* You will never plateau and become sinless in your Christian life here on earth. 1 John 1:8 clearly supports this fact: *"If we say we have no sin, we deceive ourselves, and the truth is not in us."* John is not addressing non believers who only sin before they are converted, as some would have us to believe. He says **"we."** He is writing to believers in Jesus Christ.

But here is something very comforting. Paul, in Romans 6, teaches us about the birth of the new man and then he moves on in Romans 7 to discuss the internal work of the Holy Spirit in our mortifying the deeds of our flesh. He then soars to the very pinnacle of the New Testament in Romans 8 by introducing us to justification by faith and His sanctifying work in us. Why does he sandwich Romans 7 in the middle? To tell you that, in spite of all these great and glorious things God has done and is doing, you are still trapped in a body where sin does exist. You are human! Paul at the end of his life viewed himself as chief among sinners (1 Timothy 1:15). He asserted his own fallen state when he said that he longed for the day when he would leave his body and be with the Lord. Then, he heralded, he would finally arrive at a state of true sinless perfection.

Cut Off on the Outside Only?

A second point that Romans 8:13 does not infer is **the mere internalizing of sin**. In other words, simply cutting off a sin on the outside of your life, but continuing to harbor it in your mind. This is not to be done. John Owen years ago said, "He that is appointed to kill an enemy, if he stops striking the enemy before the enemy ceases living, he has only done half the work." That is the case here. You've got to strike sin until it's dead. Don't just keep it from public view. If you allow it to stay inside in your mind, your imagination will easily take over, illuminate it and cause it to be acted out again. The sin will eventually resurface.

To illustrate this point, I'll share an experience I had doing horticultural work on a farm in Oregon years ago. Having grown up in Southern California, I wasn't used to five and six acre gardens. In fact, up to that time, my closest contact with a garden was the local vegetable department in the supermarket.

My assignment was to weed a six acre plot using a tool with a forked end. I was to stick the tool deep into the ground and pull up the roots along with the weed. Well, let me tell you that some of the thistles that grow in the summer up there are gigantic! The roots are deep and it's tough to get it all out. I decided I needed to find a faster way to eliminate the weeds than by using this little tool. And I did. Once my supervisor left, I sped up this weed–picking process. I just yanked off the top of the weed and moved on, throwing the discarded weeds in a bag. I made record time. No weeds were left.

The supervisor soon came around again, noticed the weeds were gone and complimented me on my *hard work*. "It was just the Lord," I confidently said, all the time hiding the fact I had really done a sloppy job just to get it out of the way. The problem was this: within a few days, all the weeds were back! My supervisor took me to the garden and said, "Just the Lord, huh?" I stammered, embarrassed by what I had done. He told me that to effectively get rid of a weed, I must get the root out. So it is with sin. If we internalize it, just chop it off on the outside, it is still inside and will eventually surface again. This is why Romans 12:2 tells us we are to be *"transformed by the renewing of your mind."* This is done with the Word of God. (More on this later.)

Is This a Sin Exchange Program?

Romans 8:13 is also not referring to **merely exchanging one sin for another**. That would be like adopting a spiritual methadone program. If you were hooked on heroin, for example, and couldn't get off, the doctors will prescribe methadone, a synthetic narcotic that is not as addictive as heroin. But it is addictive. All that is accomplished is substituting one habit for another; one drug taking the place of the first. Your problem is not cured. You are now an addict on methadone instead of heroin. You are still an addict and enslaved to a drug.

Sometimes we rationalize and try to convince ourselves that we aren't doing "that sin" anymore. But what we really did was replace that one action with another, having the same result, just a different sin.

A Temporary Random Shock Victory?

Putting sin to death, is also not what I would call **a random shock victory**. This is when God abruptly deals with sin in your life. You are shocked, feel "found out" by Him, beg God for forgiveness and vow that you will never do this sin again. The problem is that you are more concerned about being caught, than you are of repenting from the sin. That is no victory at all. In reality, that sin is like a thief who has been caught and now is laying low until the heat blows over. His behavior has not changed.

We find the children of Israel exemplifying this same trait in the Old Testament. They were not responding to God's chastening, so He shocked them by suddenly moving in on the sin.

> *In spite of this they still sinned, and did not*
> *believe in His wondrous works. Therefore their*
> *days He consumed in futility, and their years in*
> *fear. When He slew them, then they sought Him;*
> *And they returned and sought earnestly for God.*
> *Then they remembered that God was their rock,*
> *and the Most High God their Redeemer.*
> *Nevertheless they flattered Him with their*
> *mouth, and they lied to Him with their tongue;*
> *For their heart was not steadfast with Him, nor*
> *were they faithful in His covenant.*
>
> —Psalm 78:32–37

Notice that it was only when He began
punishing them by execution that, in their shock,
they earnestly sought forgiveness and returned
to Him. They finally remembered God was their
Rock and Redeemer. Unfortunately, it didn't
last. Only after God started killing a number of
them in punishment for their sin, did they turn
to Him. In shock, they recoiled and figured they
had better seek God, claiming Him as their
Rock. But in reality, they were far from Him in
their hearts and had no intentions of changing.

Pressure From the Outside to Clean Up the Inside?

Lastly, mortification of sin is not **an outward process**. We cannot change ourselves on the inside by applying outward pressure. Paul states in Romans 8:13, *"if by the spirit you put to death the deeds of the body, you will live."* It is impossible to put sin to death in your life through outward physical methods.

Throughout Church history, though, many well intentioned believers were deceived and did strange things in an attempt to eliminate sin. Hundreds of people during the 4th Century, for example, thought they would become more holy if they punished their bodies by living as hermits, attempting to escape the gratification of their physical lusts. A man named St. Ascepsamus wore so many chains on his body that he had to crawl around everywhere on his hands and knees. A monk named Basarian refused to lay down for forty years, so that he would not give in to his body's desire for restful sleep. Macarious the Younger sat naked in a swamp for six months and Saint Maron spent 11 years in a hollowed out tree trunk. Others lived in caves and dens of beasts, dry wells and tombs, suffering the discomfort of filth, stench, worms and maggots. All these things were considered to be spiritually beneficial and a sign of victory over the body. Even Martin Luther, before he discovered salvation by grace, had participated in this kind of activity.

Agnes de Rochier, the only daughter of a wealthy merchant in Paris, however, exemplifies one of the saddest of cases. Admired by all for her beauty and virtue, she was considered a wonderful young woman. In 1403 her father died, leaving her as the sole possessor of his wealth. False rumors soon circulated of amorous encounters. Desiring to be known as a virtuous, godly woman, she determined to spend the remainder of her days as a recluse in a narrow cell built in the wall of the Church of St. Opportune. Agnes entered her final abode, a space only a few feet square, on October 5th. The Bishop of Paris, attended by his chaplains and the cannons of Notre Dame, entered the cell, celebrated a pontifical mass, then sprinkled its opening with holy water. After bidding adieu to her friends and relatives, she ordered the masons to finish their work. No opening remained except a small hole through which Agnes might hear the church services and receive things given to her by charitable people. She was eighteen years old when she entered her living tomb and died within it eighty years later. What a tragedy!

We must guard ourselves from self-deception and, especially, a lack of understanding of God's Word. We need a balanced approach to overcoming sin and enjoying God. We must learn to deal with the sin problem from within. Jesus makes this fact very clear.

> *But those things which proceed out of the mouth come from the heart, and they defile a man. For out of the heart proceed evil thoughts, murders, adulteries, fornications, thefts, false witness, blasphemies. These are the things which defile a man, but to eat with unwashed hands does not defile a man.*
>
> —Matthew 15:18–20

The Jews in that day were led by outward purification thinking. Their problem, though they did not realize it, was that their hearts were left unchanged. Jesus is saying that you have to deal with the heart. Sin is a matter of the heart and must be dealt with on the inside.

CHAPTER 5

TIME FOR A WORKING DEFINITION

Habits

Now that we understand what mortification is not, let's review what it is and its goal. Its definition: **to mortify sin is to put sin to death; or, basically, to remove its strength from your life.** It relates to the habitual weakening of sin in your life and your daily battle against it, achieving a measure of ongoing success. Simply put, mortification is all about eliminating old sinful habits, cultivating and replacing them with new righteous practices. In a very real sense, we are talking in this book about the power of habits, for bad or for good. Someone has written these words:

You may know me.
I'm your constant companion.
I'm your greatest helper;
I'm your heaviest burden.
I will push you onward
or drag you down to failure.
I am at your command.
Half the tasks you do might as well
be turned over to me.
I'm able to do them quickly, and I'm able to do
them the same every time if that's what you want.
I'm easily managed,
all you've got to do is be firm with me.
Show me exactly how you want it done; after a
few lessons I'll do it automatically.
I am the servant of all great men and women; of
course, servant of the failures as well.
I've made all the great individuals
who have ever been great.
And I've made all the failures, too.
But I work with all the precision of a marvelous
computer with the intelligence of a human being.
Take me. Be easy with me and I will destroy you.
Be firm with me
and I'll put the world at your feet.

Who am I?

I'm Habit!

Paul is referring to the abundant Christian life here and now on earth for all believers.

For he who sows to his flesh will of the flesh reap corruption, but he who sows to the Spirit will of the Spirit reap everlasting life.
—Galatians 6:8

In this process of overcoming sin, you no longer allow it to boss you around. But it is a constant battle. Still, remember this: **not all sin is besetting sin.** A besetting sin is sometimes called a life sin, something that may have bothered you your entire life. Generally speaking, each of us is bothered by only a couple sins that always seem to bombard our minds. Not all sin is like that. Many of our sins can be dealt with quickly and fairly easily.

For example, from about the 4th grade on, all my friends at school began cussing and spitting. So I began to cuss and spit. They also started smoking behind the grammar school buildings. These became habits in our lives and just continued through the years. But when I came to Christ, I found that it was not that difficult to give up some of these outward sins. I simply just stopped cussing and spitting. Does that mean that the cussing doesn't echo in your mind for years afterwards? No, it still does. But as it comes into your mind, do you entertain it? No, you cast it down! Always deal with these besetting sins first, placing them before the throne of God. Ask Him to give you the strength and wait on Him for the victory. In Him, you will prevail in His time. Meanwhile, develop that intimate relationship with your Lord, and praise Him for the victories, great and small.

Our attitude should be like Caleb, one of several spies Joshua sent to scout the Promised Land. Upon their return, exciting reports were given about its lushness and provision—grapes, milk, honey, fruit and nuts. But they also saw giants in the land. God's people reacted with great fear and, as reported in Numbers 13:30, Caleb had to quiet the people down from their wailing. He told them that they were well able to overcome the walled cities, the enemies, even the giants, and could take possession. But they only remained fearful and wept all night. Compared to those giants, they were, in their own sight, no more than grasshoppers. They forgot about how awesome God is, that it was He Who delivered them from Egypt, protected them all along and that He would continue to do so. They did not exercise faith, which barred them from entering the Promised Land.

God help us. Yes, there are giants; but there also are a lot of things that aren't giants and can be overcome along the way. We, too, are well able to go in and take the land. Let's come to God and thank Him for what He has done. Let's cultivate and enjoy our relationship with Him. Let's work on what we can while continuing to pound against your modern day giants—those old besetting sins. Eventually, they will topple and come down.

This process is like knocking down a big old building. Day after day the wrecking ball pounds the wall thousands of times in an effort to demolish it. Eventually, **a final blow** brings it down. This is how we have to look at the giant besetting sins in our lives. Come to God, pray about them, strike another blow every day. Some fall sooner than others. Don't despair if it's later. While you wait on Him, remember that you have a God who loves you dearly. The true and living God has given you a standing in Christ that is perfect, His very own righteousness in Jesus Christ. This is your position before Him. Practically, you will go on to conquer the land. It is being accomplished at

the pace which the Holy Spirit enables. Seek to
have an honest heart and never use His grace as
a cloak for sin, by abusing God's awesome gift.
Thank Him for the things that have been
conquered and continue to bring to Him the big
areas that haven't yet fallen, knowing that one
day they too will topple.

Let me encourage you with a great thought.
Not one besetting sin will follow you into
heaven. Be content with who you are, a sinner
saved by grace. You have a standing in Christ,
clothed in His robes of His righteousness. God
accepts you right now and loves you exactly as
you are. He has a plan to work through your life
and will finish what He has begun. In that
moment of time, you will be changed into the
glory of Jesus Christ. That will be permanent
sanctification and it continues forever. With that
hope firmly entrenched in your mind, move
forward to overcome sin and enjoy God.

CHAPTER 6

A BELIEVER'S EFFORT

Imagine yourself walking down a dimly lit street. It's late at night just after a rain. Puddles are everywhere. Suddenly, a car whizzes by, hits a puddle and splashes mud all over you. You stop, glance at your clothing in the dark and mumble to yourself, "Oh my, I've got mud on me; but it doesn't look too bad." You walk toward a street light some 50 yards away. Straining to see your clothes in the light's dim reflection, you think, "You know, I don't think it's too bad." But as you approach the light, you finally see the truth. It is really bad! "Man, this is so bad I have to go home and change my clothes!" This is what happens to us as we get closer and closer to Jesus and His great light!

You walk with Christ. In the beginning you're thrilled just to be forgiven of your sin. This fills your mind and thinking. You are in ecstasy with the greatest reality in life: to be forgiven and saved by God. Years roll by and you're still walking with the Lord, ever growing closer to Him. Practically speaking, you begin to realize that sin is within you. Sometimes that sin splashes all over you and muddies up your life. You acknowledge your need to change and get the sin out of your life. Daily, it becomes a wonderful obsessive quest, something you are involved in continuously. It becomes a preoccupation. You want to put to death the misdeeds of the body—sin. Why? Because you love Jesus Christ so much that you don't want anything in your life to separate you from Him. You don't want anything "jamming" your spiritual frequencies, because fellowship with Jesus is so precious and you want it to remain unbroken.

We understand that the goal of mortification of sin is to put it to death in your life. Then you can appropriate and enjoy what is yours as a Christian. We have also examined the confusion that revolves around this process in our lives. Putting sin to death is not the final elimination of sin. Nor is it merely an internalizing of sin, or an exchange of one sin for another. Further, it also is not a random shock victory where you feel like you have been "found out," and you vow to God that you will never do that trespass ever again. Nor can we overcome sin by any outward influence. We overcome it only by the influence of God within us.

"For if you live according to the flesh you will die; but if by the Spirit **you put to death the deeds of the body** *..."* Notice that an **effort** is made. *You* put to death the deeds of the body, then you will live. You must do it, and that can only be done by the Spirit. An effort is necessary; but only a believer can effectively make it. An unregenerate person has no ability at all to do this. Conversion is absolutely necessary first.

If, for example, you were a builder, you know that a good foundation must be laid before construction begins. That is what is needed here, a good foundation. Jesus Christ is that foundation. If you do not have the life of God within, you cannot successfully make the effort to eliminate sin. If you try, you will become very frustrated. This accounts for many who have left the faith. They are frustrated and want nothing further to do with Christianity. Unfortunately, they are frustrated because they wrongly approached their fight with sin.

In Acts 2:37, Peter is preaching to the multitudes. He is effective, his words penetrate deep into their hearts. *"Now when they heard this, they were cut to the heart,"* the Bible says. As deep as it could go, it went. They said to Peter and the rest of the apostles, *"Men and brethren, what shall we do?"* They felt doomed. How did Peter respond? Well, he did not tell them to first start putting sin to death in their lives and live. He didn't tell them to conquer that sin, clean up their lives, and live differently. No, he started where you have to start. In verse 38, he tells them to **repent and be baptized in the Name of Jesus Christ** for the remission of sins. Then they would receive the gift of the Holy Spirit. Peter understood their condition and that the way to freedom is only by the way of conversion. Turn away from your sin, come to Christ, and He will give you the same power. If you don't, you will fail and, in the end, probably walk away from Christ. You must start with a true conversion.

I have seen so many people come and go through the years. They are enthusiastic for a while. They enjoy the praise music. They even agree with the truths of the Gospel. They have what could be termed an orthodox belief. They accept the fact that Christ died for their sins and rose again from the dead. They enjoy attending church and, in the process of becoming a churchgoer, begin to fine–tune their lives. A few changes are made. Perhaps they drink a little less, spend a little less, or carouse a little less, but there aren't major changes. They are very small changes and, unfortunately, appear to them as proof that they are "getting into Christianity." If you ask them how they're doing, they reply that they are into this "church thing" and their lives are getting better.

I always become nervous when I hear that because the goal is **not** to "get into a church thing and do a little better." One doesn't "get into" Christianity. **It gets into you!** The goal is to personally know Jesus Christ and be radically transformed by that relationship. If you aren't converted, you will only grow worse. You may believe the right things and, as a result, even try to make changes. But if you don't know Christ personally and He isn't your life's driving force to make the needed changes, you will never see them become permanent. When you discover that no major changes have occurred in your life, you will become frustrated, bitter, uptight, and angry. You will eventually just disappear. You will no long be with Christians and if asked, "what happened?" the typical answer will be, "I tried to get into "**it**," and I couldn't live up to "**it**." I tried to be a Christian and it's too hard. I guess I'm just not cut out to be a Christian."

Everybody Qualifies

Well, the Bible says that God is the God who justifies the ungodly. If you are ungodly, you qualify. Everyone on planet Earth is ungodly, so everybody qualifies. This failure mind–set is tragic because the despair that is felt often plunges them deeper into sin than they had ever been before. They end up more hard hearted toward the Gospel and are now more unreachable than most people who have never heard the truth. True change comes only after being born again.

You must go all the way to a personal relationship with Jesus Christ. You must ask Him into your life, seek to know Him personally, and come to know that He lives within you. That is the believer's effort. If you are just a "church person" who, when asked if you are a Christian, responds that you are a Lutheran, Baptist, Catholic, or any other denomination, that is not enough. But, if you respond **with a knowing heart**, "I know Christ, have been born again, forgiven by His blood, death and resurrection and have new life in Him," then you have given the only true answer. Be sure you live it out every day.

This is the only way to begin to overcome sin in your life. First, you must be forgiven for your sin, go on to overcome it, and then enjoy freedom from it in the way you live. You can enjoy your life as a human being, having a loving relationship with your God. It begins with a believer's effort. Be very clear on this truth.

The unbeliever's inability is very significant; but so is, by contrast, the ability of the truly converted. Several reasons exist for this. As you read through the Bible you notice many commands. *"He that stole, let him steal no more,"* for instance. In other words, just stop it! You read about those in the Bible who won't go to Heaven: adulterers, idolaters, fornicators, homosexuals, they that are covetous and many others. Then you read, *"but such **were** some of* *you."* This teaches that all of us, if born again, had been in one or more of these categories, but are now changed. We now live differently and are on our way to Heaven. What's the difference? The Spirit of God did it. If you ponder on these commands, you soon realize that it is the work of living men and women to kill sin in their lives **by the power of the Holy Spirit.**

To understand living the victorious life in Christ, you must first understand the bondage of the **"old man"**—the Biblical term for the **old self.** In other words, realize how shackled to sin you really were prior to receiving Christ and becoming born again. Paul taught this truth clearly:

> *Knowing this, that our old man was crucified with Him, that the body of sin might be done away with, that we should no longer be slaves of sin.*
>
> —Romans 6:6

This speaks of the old man as having been a slave of sin. To best understand the freedom you have in Christ, you first must understand the bondage you had really been under. The old self, that which you were before you became a

Christian, was a slave of sin. In this sense, you were under sin's domination. The old you had an unbroken relationship to sin. Picture your old self woven together with the sin that lies within you—within the very fabric of your being, an inseparable connection. Salvation, however, changes all of that. The old man dies and with it the bondage you were under.

The Bible says that if you are truly born again, your former self has been crucified; it has been put to death! This is life changing truth. Romans 6:6, again, says *"knowing this that our old man was crucified with Him."* This is **past tense**. It is a once for all act that God performs in you. He sets you free from sin by first putting to death the old you. Sin has no claim upon you as it once had. A new freedom comes as a direct result of the old man in you dying. It is very important for all of us to grasp the fact that the old man **"was"** crucified. It is a completed act.

The Dog Collar

Most of us are familiar with the process of training a dog. We begin by placing a collar and leash around the dog's neck. By holding on to the collar you can give a command, while applying pressure with the other hand.

After many repetitions of these steps, you can train it to do just about any trick or act of discipline. Over a period of time the dog will become so conditioned to the whole command process, that he obeys almost without thinking. Then the day comes when you can take off the collar and he is so thoroughly trained that even without the collar, he will obey upon command.

The dog doesn't realize that once the collar is removed, he really doesn't have to obey, but because of the conditioning, he responds instantly. It is just the same in the life of the Christian. We are now free to say no. We don't have to obey the devil. We are free to say no to sin and yes to Jesus. If we do otherwise, it is because of our former conditioning.

When the old man dies, the old you is gone, but the sin is still there. The sin, that force within your humanness in your body, still resides and has not changed even one bit. **You have changed**, but the sin force within you hasn't. Paul calls this the *"sin that lies within..."* A brand new creature replaces the old man and continues on in salvation. We can live differently because of the great work that God does in us.

If indeed you have heard Him and have been taught by Him, as the truth is in Jesus: that you put off concerning your former conduct...
—Ephesians 4:21–22

That's the old man which produced a conduct in your old life that grew corrupt because of deceitful lusts. An unbeliever is left to the influence of his own sin and will only grow worse throughout his life. If you don't know Jesus, you can look at your past and view a downward spiral. You are getting worse and not getting better. The old man daily grows more corrupt.

The Christian, in contrast, has had this old man die. Therefore, the power is available to put off the conduct of the old man and live a life in keeping with the new man. He is being renewed in the spirit of his mind. That is what we are experiencing right now—being renewed in the truth of what God has done to us and in us. Be renewed in the spirit of **your** mind by living in accordance with the new man, which was created according to God.

Not only did a crucifixion take place, there was also a new creation. In what way is the new you created according to God? You are created in true righteousness and holiness. That is the reason a newborn babe in Christ has holy longings. In Romans 8, Paul refers to it as "Abba, Father." From the first moment of your salvation, something inside of you cries out to God to be near Him. It is a brand new you. Your old self had sinful longings; but the brand new you has holy longings "created according to God, in true righteousness and holiness" (Ephesians 4:24).

Charles Wesley described this great freedom of the new birth in one his hymns.

Long my imprisoned spirit lay
Fast bound in sin in natures night;
Thine eye defused a quick'ning ray
I woke, the dungeon flamed with light;
My chains fell off, my heart was free;
I rose went forth and followed Thee.

It is because of this new found freedom in Christ that Paul is realistically able to exhort us to put off specific sins. In Colossians, Paul lists specific sins that we are to eliminate. Beginning in Colossians 3:5–6, Paul writes,

Mortify therefore your members which are upon
the earth; fornication, uncleanness, inordinate

affection, evil concupiscence, and covetousness, which is idolatry: for which things' sake the wrath of God cometh on the children of disobedience.

He continues the list in verse 8,

But now ye also put off all these: anger, wrath, malice, blasphemy, filthy communication out of your mouth. Lie not one to another, seeing that ye have put off the old man with his deeds; and have put on the new man, which is renewed in knowledge after the image of him that created him. (KJV)

People do not commit general sins. They carry out specific ones. So, Paul writes against specific sins that are to be stopped, and then provides the reason why that can successfully be done.

Do not lie to one another, since you have put off the old man with his deeds, and have put on the new man who is renewed in knowledge according to the image of Him who created him.
—Colossians 3:9–10

I love studying the Word of God because it feeds the new man with Scriptural knowledge. Nothing can energize you better. Be encouraged and strengthened to move forward in this victorious Christian life.

Jesus came, rescued you, and severed the union that sin had to you. He put to death the old man, then recreated you in a way where the old sin connection can never be fully reconnected. You are now connected in a new way. **Grasp this truth: as a Christian, you are now in a superior position over sin and have the ability to say no to it.** You could not do this before. Because you can now say no to sin, you are free from its bondage. Sin is still present in your body; it resides within your humanness. But, as Paul said,

> It is no longer I who do it, but sin that dwells in me.
>
> —Romans 7:17

The **new *I*** is created after God in righteous and true holiness. You don't want to sin anymore, but sin exists within you. Keep a close watch or you can be deceived and tripped up. Sin temporarily gets reconnected and influences you. It does still lie within, but no longer can maintain control. That is the difference. Its reign and dominance over you have been broken, though sin's presence is intact. It is still there, unchanged; but that old man who once was under its complete dominion is now dead and is no longer influenced by its corruption. The new man in you is now forever connected with the Holy Spirit who lives inside you.

Therefore, when you fall into sin, you will eventually get back up and keep going. That's why Satan cannot have full victory over you. That's why you can never go back to your old life and enjoy it. I am convinced that is also the reason why people who have supposedly backslid for years, have really lived unconverted lives all along. A true born again child of God is fused with the Holy Spirit and His dominating power. He energizes you to continue your walk with Christ and causes your life to change. You will eventually find victory in areas of your life you thought could never be. Then you realize the superiority of the new man over sin.

Dead to Sin and Alive to Christ

In Romans 6:11, Paul articulates these truths:

Likewise you also, reckon yourselves to be dead indeed to sin, but alive to God in Jesus Christ our Lord.

To me, that is one of the greatest statements

in the Bible. We live in a tempting world, but we are dead to sin and alive to Christ! This is a wonderful thought. Meditate upon it and always hide it in your heart. Repeat it daily as long as you live: *"Dead to sin and alive to Christ."* You no longer allow sin to reign in your mortal body, that you should obey it and its lusts. Why? Because you don't have to any more. That cannot be said, however, for an unconverted person. Without the Holy Spirit's power within, it is hopeless to attempt to control sin.

As a believer, you must stop permitting sin to boss you around. **It isn't boss anymore!** Paul reinforces this when, in Romans 6:13 he says,

> *And do not present your members as instruments of unrighteousness to sin, but present yourselves to God as being alive from the dead.*

Just as sin once dominated the old you and controlled what you did with your body, the Holy Spirit now governs the new you. Consequently, you should allow Him to direct what you do with your body. You are now the temple of the Holy Spirit; let Him have free reign. Submit to His promptings and live in accordance with what He is doing in your life. Present yourselves to God as being alive from the dead and your members as instruments of righteousness to Him.

> *For sin shall not have dominion over you, for you are not under law but under grace.*
>
> —Romans 6:14

You have been saved by grace. That brings about a transformation. You are a new creature in Christ; the old you is dead. Live like it and enjoy it. That is what Paul is saying. In truth, how you conduct yourself, in speech or in deed, reflects the fact that you are or are not walking in the power and influence of the Holy Spirit. He must be the dominating influence in your life.

The new you is a totally different type of person than you were before. You cannot be held under sin's unbroken dominance any longer. Though sin still resides within, you now have the superiority. And so, Paul writes in Romans 6:6, *"knowing this, that our old man was crucified with Him, that the body of sin might be done away with, that we should no longer be slaves of sin."* J.B. Phillips translates the same verse this way: *"Let us never forget that our old selves died with Him on the cross and that the tyranny of sin over us might be broken."* What wonderful reassurance of God's grace to you!

What is the secret of your superiority over sin's tyranny? It is the unbroken union that you have with the Holy Spirit in Jesus Christ. Paul masterfully sums this up in Galatians 2:20: *"I have been crucified with Christ, it is no longer I who live,"* (My old man is dead.) *"...but Christ lives in me; and the life which I now live..."* (Notice it isn't just Christ in Paul's body; he says, *"the life which I now live."* A new *I* rises up and is joined to Christ.) *"Christ lives in me; and the life which I now live in the flesh I live by faith in the Son of God, who loved me and gave Himself for me."* You are a new creature. A new you exists within and that new creation is joined to Jesus Christ and lives a new life by faith.

William Newell, in his commentary on Romans, applauds the truth about the death of the old man. He says, "There is nothing in all of the Bible that requires a more constant, vigilant attention than that truth." Why? Because those words are addressed to faith. You receive Christ in faith; the old mans dies and a new man is born. But your feelings can fool you. Feelings can betray you. Don't trust them until you have peace in your heart and everything lines up with the Word of God. Learn to walk by faith anchored in the Word of God; not according to your feelings alone. **Our faith is anchored in this fact: that the old man is dead and we are no longer slaves to sin.**

The life that you now live is joined to Jesus Christ and is to be lived through His power— one day at a time. You can enjoy victory by His power because He is working within you. God declared this promise long ago to His people in the Book of Ezekiel:

> *I will give you a new heart and put a new spirit within you; I will take the heart of stone out of your flesh and give you a heart of flesh. I will put My Spirit within you and cause you to walk in My statutes, and you will keep My judgments and do them.*

—Ezekiel 36:26–27

That is the old man, who was hardened toward God and insensitive to His touch, dying. God has put a new heart within you, sensitive to His touch, and then sent His Spirit to live within you.

Notice the many commands addressed to you as a new creature? Concerned that you can't do them? Don't be. God tells you what to do and what not to do. And here is the secret: **God will cause you to walk in His statutes. He will do it**

within you through His power. Why? Because
you are His brand new creation, and with His
power you will be able to do these things and
keep His judgments. And to give you added
confidence, He reassures you in Isaiah 40:29 that
He gives power to the weak. That is very
comforting because we all qualify. We are all
weak and need His strength and power.

Do you feel weak? Then you feel like all the
rest of us! His power is available for you and
will increase your strength, as God comes to
you, a hopeless, helpless and lost human being,
bound in sin, and frees you. He finds and
rescues you, changes you inside and out, and
gives you might and strength to live a joyous
Christian life. You learn to know and love Him;
discover His truths and that His commands are
not grievous. You obey Him because you love to
walk in His light and have fellowship with Him.
You enjoy being free from the sin that once
wrecked your life. It is a joy to overcome sin and
enjoy God. It is the greatest thrill of one's life. It
is the only way to live life as a Christian.

CHAPTER 7

TAPPING INTO HIS POWER

Integral to our necessary effort is that it must be led by the Spirit of God. *"If by the Spirit you put to death the deeds of the body, you will live."* The power to overcome any sin must come from the Holy Spirit. God has given us His presence and power in abundance. Jesus said that His Father would give you the Spirit in abundance if you would only come to Him. He will manifest His presence. *"How much more will your heavenly Father give the Holy Spirit to those who ask Him"* (Luke 11:13).

He Produces His Own Fruit

The Holy Spirit comes to abide with you forever and cultivates His fruit in you. This is one way we can eliminate sin from our lives.

The Bible, however, teaches that the flesh, the sin within you, also spawns fruit. Galatians 5:19–21 details a dreadful list of the sins of the flesh. In contrast, the Spirit also produces fruit once He enters your life and works His sanctifying grace in you.

> *But the fruit of the Spirit is love, joy, peace, long–suffering, kindness, goodness, faithfulness, gentleness, self–control. Against such there is no law.*
>
> —Galatians 5:22–23

It is encouraging to know that the Spirit of God weeds out the sin and replaces it with His own good fruit. That is one of the reasons that the Christian can be so different when he lives the Spirit filled life.

When the Spirit is not grieved by your life, He continues to bring forth His fruit in abundance. *"A sower went out to sow...[the seed that] fell on good ground and yielded a crop: some a hundredfold, some sixty, some thirty"* (Matthew 13:3,8). The fruit that your life bears comes according to the nature of the life you live.

He Gives You a Hatred for Sin

The Holy Spirit also gives us a hatred for

sin. You can review your pre–Christian life and realize that you loved sin. But because you now belong to Him, you hate the sin. That is because the old man died and the new man was born. I can attest to this in my own life.

Before I was born again, I loved sin. I didn't care too much for its consequences, but I loved the sin. Living in darkness, I hated the law of God, didn't want to hear anything about it or what He required of me. At my new birth, however, something radically changed within me. Now I hate my sin and love the Word of God, the revelation of God's truth. Now I know and appreciate that His revelation, the Bible, brings me near to Him.

Thomas Brooks years ago explained it this way: "The first work of the Spirit is to make a man look upon sin as an enemy, to deal with sin as an enemy, to hate it as an enemy, to loath it as an enemy and then to arm against it as an enemy." We are in a death match with sin. It wars against our very souls to enslave us. We must arm ourselves if we are to be victorious. To hate sin is the first positive step in winning the war. Turn from it and get it out of your life.

He Works With Your Cooperation

The Holy Spirit, with your cooperation, works all this within you—*"to will and to do for His good pleasure"* (Philippians 2:13). He is the reason you want to turn from sin. *"If by the Spirit you put to death the deeds of the body."* You shirk the apathy and indifference so many others display, take responsibility for change in your life, and get involved. You *will* to get involved.

In the book of Philippians, Paul couples together the effort of the believer and the work of God's Spirit within you. If you are ever going to grow and change, these two must be present in your life.

> *Therefore, my beloved, as you have always obeyed, not as in my presence only, but now much more in my absence, work out your own salvation with fear and trembling.*
> —Philippians 2:12

The great Apostle is not encouraging you to save yourself. He is instructing you to work out in your life what God is working within you—a productive and victorious life. He says, *"For it is God who works in you both to will and to do for His good pleasure"* (Philippians 2:13). He is saying to get in step with the work of the Spirit within you. Work together with Him.

If you are to overcome sin, you must implement the truth of cooperating with the Holy Spirit. The great Comforter works **in and with you** for the mortification of sin in your life. He will never work against you, nor does He work without you. Without your involvement linked with His influence and power, you will never change and become holy.

It is like the old deacon who frequently led Wednesday evening prayer meetings and always concluded them with the petition, "Oh, Lord, clean out all the cobwebs in my life." This continued for a long time. A neighbor of his, who also attended the prayer meetings, knew the deacon to be quite carnal and refused to take responsibility to change his sin. The neighbor became very irritated with the deacon's closing phrase. Finally, one Wednesday night, as the deacon in his usual manner began his closing phrase, "Oh Lord, take out all the cobwebs of sin in my life," the frustrated neighbor jumped to his feet and shouted, "Don't do it Lord, don't do it! Make him kill the spider!"

You must cooperate with the Holy Spirit to

see change. *"If by the Spirit you put to death the deeds of the body, you will live."* Be willing to change in any area of your life. Only God knows all the areas that need to change. Don't refuse Him entrance to any area. That grieves the Holy Spirit. All sin is bad, and you must not compartmentalize any section of your life.

The Bible is very clear that there is **short–term** pleasure in sin. Don't be duped and think otherwise. Even playing with sin is like trying to pet a scorpion. It will sting and kill you. Remember, one sin always makes way for another. Each time sin manifests itself, it is with the intent to completely enslave you and kill your fellowship with the Lord. If you wall off your life in certain areas, you are allowing sin to creep into every other area that you supposedly offer to God.

Thieves understand this kind of dynamic. In our house we have big and small windows. I have always been careful to lock the large ones, but never concerned myself with the little ones. Then I discovered that thieves look for houses that have small unlocked windows to break into. How can a full–sized adult do that? They don't. They use a small child who can fit through the little window. The child is helped through the opening, then runs around and opens the front door. The adult thieves then have full reign in the home to steal whatever they want.

That is how sin works in your life. It only takes one little sin to unlock the door for bigger sins to enter other compartments in your life and ruin it. John Owen had this in mind as he said,

> Give yourself to the mortification of sin, make it your daily work, be always at it while you live. Cease not a day from this work. Be killing sin or it will be killing you.

If you want your life to have joy, the peace that passes understanding, and love that knows no depths, then you must bring every area of your life to God. Ask Him to have His way in you and hold nothing back. Even if you are unwilling, ask Him to make you willing.

> *Therefore, having these promises, beloved, let us cleanse ourselves from all filthiness of the flesh and spirit, perfecting holiness in the fear of God.*
> —2 Corinthians 7:1

Paul sets the standard as to the kind of people we should be. Make it your life's work to perfect holiness in the fear of God.

CHAPTER 8

THE PRACTICAL STEPS I CAN NOW TAKE

1. Reckon the Old Man Dead

As you earnestly look at how to practically overcome sin, you must reckon the old man dead. Exercise the truth of Romans 6, that you are no longer who you used to be. You are not the same person if you are born again. God has re–created you and has made you new in Christ. All the old things are passed away and all things have become new. Stand on that truth. The Bible calls it, *"reckoning the old man dead."* This isn't a casual or light–weight issue. It is a clearly articulated truth in God's Word. Your old life is dead and you are a new creature in Christ. Always live with that in mind.

As Christians, we often confront problems

or sins and seem to wait for a thunderbolt from Heaven to strike that area and change it. We really need only to reckon that area of our life dead and walk in that truth. This is exactly what Paul taught in Romans.

> *Likewise you also, reckon yourselves to be dead indeed to sin, but alive to God in Christ Jesus our Lord. Therefore do not let sin reign in your mortal body, that you should obey it in its lusts. And do not present your members as instruments of unrighteousness to sin, but present yourselves to God as being alive from the dead, and your members as instruments of righteousness to God. For sin shall not have dominion over you, for you are not under law but under grace.*
>
> —Romans 6:11–14

Notice that he doesn't say to wait for a thunderbolt. Paul simply says to stop living as you have been, using your body in unrighteous behavior. Instead, begin giving your body to God for righteousness and live as though you have risen from the dead with Christ. You are born again. Start now! Reckoning the old man dead is the first practical step you must take.

2. No Provision for the Flesh

Secondly, **make no provision for your flesh.**

Those who do not know Christ live in sin, love its ways and hate God's law. They make provision for sin. For the Christian, however, Romans 13:14 states, *"But put on the Lord Jesus Christ, and make no provision for the flesh, to fulfill its lusts."* After 13 Chapters of teaching in Romans, Paul says not to provide any entry point for sin. All that you learn about scheming to sin, stop it! Get it out of your life! Make no provision for sin! Exercise self–control so that you can deny the flesh.

Think about the damage sin does in your life if you leave it unchecked. Think about how much damage it has done in the past. Be a long–range thinker and you will be motivated to exercise self–control and make no provision for the flesh. This is stated clearly in 1 Peter 2:11:

> *Beloved, I beg you as sojourners and pilgrims, abstain from fleshly lusts which war against the soul.*

Yes, there is pleasure in sin **for a season**, but don't forget that sin is at war against your soul. It wants to rob you of everything that you dearly love in life. John Owen said, "Sin is not only present, but active. If not mortified, it will bring great cursed, scandalous soul destroying sins.

Sins that are not killed will weaken the spirit, destroy the vigor of the soul, and weaken it for all duties in the Christian life. It will darken the soul by hiding the love of God and remove the sense of adoptive privilege." In other words, sin is active and, if you don't do something about it, it will strip you of God's love in your soul.

This is the reason we see fewer people productive in the Body of Christ. Sin causes you to be apathetic, indifferent and numb to sermons and exhortations. It anesthetizes you to Bible study and even the love of God's people. It makes you not want the godly counsel a pastor can give. It strips you of life, and it leaves you deaf, dumb and blind. Even worse, you don't care that you are deaf, dumb and blind. If you don't do something about it, it will always do something to you. We exercise self–control by making no provision for the flesh. Remember that self–control is one of the fruits of the Spirit. How do you exercise self–control? By walking in the Spirit and being sensitive to His guidance and His work in you.

Sometimes changing your lifestyle is needed to live near to God and be free from sin. Remember when Lot was living with Abraham.

Each of their flocks got too large to share grazing land. They decided to part company. Each rearranged his lifestyle. Together, they looked out over all the land. Lot, unfortunately, chose the lush plains surrounding a very sinful city called Sodom. Notice his progression: Lot first **settled near** Sodom, later **moved into the city**, and **finally sat in the very city gates as one of its leaders.** When the Lord judged Sodom and another city nearby, Gommorah, for their sin and iniquity, the Bible describes the fact that God's dispatched Angels had to take hold of Lot's hands and those of his wife and daughters and forcibly drag them out of the city! Lot had become numb by sin which, ultimately, coursed its way through his family like a cancer. He rearranged his life in the wrong direction.

You must do everything you can to stay away from sin. If you are living in adultery, you terminate the relationship. If you are a Christian and are fornicating with your Christian fiancee, stop it! Whatever the sin is, commit to change immediately. Repent of it, get on your knees and weep before God. Ask His forgiveness for your indifference and selfishness. You have cared more for your own flesh than for the glory of God. Rearrange your lifestyle and quit giving excuses. They are meaningless to God.

Do not be wise in your own eyes; Fear the Lord and depart from evil.

—Proverbs 3:7

God tells you to depart from evil because He loves you. He knows that sin left unchecked will destroy you. He loves you too much to let you rush into destruction without trying to stop you every step of the way.

There is no death of sin without the death of Jesus Christ. If you remember this truth, it will inspire you to change your lifestyle wherever necessary: He died so you could be free. Let your sinful companions know you are changing. Serve notice to your friends that you are committed to altering your lifestyle. By doing so, you are also standing up for Jesus Christ.

A young Chinese man did just that. An American preacher, ministering in a Southeast Asian country, was staying with a wealthy Chinese couple who were on–fire believers. Their adult son, however, still living at home, was an unbeliever and had been living a sinful life. One evening the minister invited him to attend a service and he agreed to come. The young man received Christ as his personal Savior. The very next day he had cards printed in English and Chinese, sending them to hundreds of his friends and acquaintances. The cards expressed the impact of a converted life: **"Wang Lee, having given his life yesterday to Jesus, His Lord and Savior, wishes to inform you that he will no longer be seen in the usual places that he has frequented."** He served notice that he was not coming back. His previous lifestyle forever changed when he came to know Jesus Christ.

What about you? The Bible says that bad company corrupts you. You must also rearrange your lifestyle and serve notice to your sinful companions that you are not going to live as you have been living any longer. You have turned from the sin and are now walking in the other direction. Simply stated, in terms of making no provision for the flesh, **if you don't want to fall, don't walk where it's slippery!**

3. Cultivate a Godly Life

A third practical thought is to **cultivate a godly life.** In other words, make a decision that you are not going to be a worldly Christian. In the past, I have lived my life as a worldly

Christian. I know what it's like. I know that this kind of lifestyle does not stop **until** you make a conscious decision not to be worldly anymore. Instead, strive to be godly and follow Jesus as closely as you can. You commit yourself to cultivate a righteous life.

4. Give Yourself to Quality Prayer Time

I think one of the most enjoyable and beneficial things we can do in life, is learn to be quiet before God. Psalm 46:10 says, *"Be still, and know that I am God."* It is much more difficult to sin when you have sat in the presence of God, and His Spirit has worked His way through every compartment of your heart. This precious time alone with your Lord is set aside for absolute honesty about the details of your life. Don't be general and vague with God. Remember, He knows it all anyway.

> *He who conceals his sins does not prosper, but whoever confesses and renounces them finds mercy.*
>
> —Proverbs 28:13 NIV

Be honest with God. Call each sin exactly what it is: **sin!** Drag your sins out into the light and give them names. Don't just say, "Lord I'm having a problem, please help me." Be specific.

For example, if all you do is think about money, confess that you are greedy. Repent of it before God. Whatever it might be, name it in front of Him. He responds to an honest repentant heart. Confess it, turn from it, receive forgiveness and walk on with Jesus. Your Lord loves and accepts you.

In Colossians 3:5–9, Paul gives us this example:

> *Therefore put to death your members which are on earth: fornication, uncleanness, passion, evil desire, and covetousness, which is idolatry. Because of these things the wrath of God is coming upon the sons of disobedience.*

He is reminding us of how much God hates these sins.

> *In which you yourselves **once walked** when you lived in them. But now you yourselves are to put off all these: anger, wrath, malice, blasphemy, filthy language out of your mouth. Do not lie to one another, since you have put off the old man with his deeds.*

He gives these sins names and says, "[You] have put on the new man who is renewed in knowledge according to the image of Him who created *him*" (Colossians 3:10). You have the power within you to change. Do it!

When was the last time you actually asked God to forgive you for doing a specific sin? Or have you become accustomed to letting it slip and don't even think about it anymore? Don't miss this important fact: **overall, God is looking for the right heart attitude; not perfection.** The perfection He wants in you has already been found in the blood of Christ that covers your life. **The heart of the matter is the matter of the heart.** Quality prayer time is a great key to overcoming sin.

5. Give Yourself to Quality Study Time

To put it very plainly, this is absolutely mandatory. If you skip your Bible reading time, you will not be victorious. You will discover that just reading at random is not quite enough to live a godly life. I suggest that you have an actual reading plan, one that will move you consistently through the Word. George Muller, at age 93, read the entire Bible through four times. At the same time, he still maintained an international ministry, having 7 people assigned just to help him with his correspondence. He was responsible for 10 churches and thousands

of orphans. Yet, he found time to read his Bible
through four times every year.

Think of George Muller the next time you
think you can't read three or four chapters a day
with your busy schedule. You need to read in
general and also study selected topics in detail.
Fill your mind with the Word of God. As a
result, you will know two important truths: God
really loves man, and He really hates man's sin.

> *In mercy and truth atonement is provided for
> iniquity; and by the fear of the Lord one departs
> from evil.*
>
> —Proverbs 16:6

As you read the Word, you see a holy God
interacting with sinful man and come away with
a fresh fear of God in your heart. Be honest and
ask for His help to be able to truly understand
that your life is under grace.

Many years ago Horatio Bonar said,

> We must study the Bible more. We must not
> only lay it up within us, but transfuse it
> through the whole texture of our soul.

Don't just read the Bible to gain head
knowledge. Bathe yourself in it until its truth
transfuses your very soul, because that is where

the changes will occur. You will find that the thrill of discovery becomes addictive and that deception is dispelled by the light of understanding. Psalm 119 tells us that God's Word is a lamp to our feet and a light to our path. If we hide His Word in our hearts, then we won't sin against Him.

> *This Book of the Law shall not depart from your mouth, but you shall meditate in it day and night, that you may observe to do according to all that is written in it. For then you will make your way prosperous, and then you will have good success.*
>
> —Joshua 1:8

Do you want to have good success at overcoming sin in your life? Fill your life with the Word of God. Read it through, study it, and apply its truths in your life. Then you will know the secret of Jesus, when He prayed to the Heavenly Father.

> *Sanctify them by Your truth: Your word is truth.*
> —John 17:17

Jesus understood the dynamic power of the Word. So many of our troubles come because we don't know the Scriptures. We do not read God's love letter to us. Sermons are great,

Christian radio is great, cassette tapes are great, but none of these things can replace reading the Bible on your own. Personally knowing God leads to overcoming sin.

The power to eliminate sin in our life occurs when we read the Bible and obey it. Cultivate a godly life through quality prayer time, quality study time, and then work very hard at one other thing:

6. Quality Time Management

We are to redeem the time God gives each of us because the days are evil. Ephesians 5:17 states, *"do not be unwise, but understand what the will of the Lord is."* **We must manage our lives by being Christ–centered.**

If you cultivate a godly life, sin can't survive. If you live by the Spirit and put to death the deeds of the body, you will live the abundant life. Take this seriously and make realistic, practical steps to do it. Begin by changing corruptive relationships and habits; order your life around your church attendance and involvement. You will begin to see everything radically change and you'll experience a whole new life in Christ. Cherish in your heart what Isaiah says:

> *You come to the help of those who gladly do right,*
> *who remember Your ways.*
>
> —Isaiah 64:5 NIV

The Lord will come to your aid and will meet and bless you in the way, as you learn to overcome sin and enjoy God.

Don't ever forget this. God understands your struggles and the pain that sin imparts. He asks you to bring your sins to Him, so He can bathe you in His mercy and grace. He wants to communicate His great love to you, as you come in honest repentant prayer.

> *As a father pities his children, so the Lord pities those who fear Him.*
>
> —Psalm 103:13

He wants an open, honest, God–fearing heart in you. When you fail and return to Him with an honest heart, He forgives, is merciful and pours His grace upon you.

The story is told of a pilot in years gone by, who was flying his small plane one day and heard a noise which he recognized as the gnawing of a rat. Wondering what its sharp teeth were cutting through, he suddenly realized with horror that it might be an electrical wire. Then he remembered that rodents can't survive at high altitudes. Immediately he began climbing until finally he had to put on his oxygen mask. Soon the gnawing sound ceased, and when he landed he found the rat—dead.

This is a tremendous analogy to overcoming sin in the Christian life. The secret is to spend your life enjoying fellowship with God. Allowing the Holy Spirit to draw you into those glorious "high altitudes" with Jesus Christ— where sin cannot survive!

How to Become a Christian

First of all you must recognize that you are a sinner. Realize that you have missed the mark. This is true of each of us. We have deliberately crossed the line not once, but many times. The Bible says, "All have sinned and fallen short of the glory of God" (Romans 3:23). This is a hard admission for many to make, but if we are not willing to hear the bad news, we cannot appreciate and respond to the *good news*.

Second, we must realize that Jesus Christ died on the cross for us. Because of sin, God had to take drastic measures to reach us. So He came to this earth and walked here as a man. But Jesus was more than just a good man. He was the God-man—God incarnate—and that is why His death on the cross is so significant.

At the cross, God Himself—in the person of Jesus Christ—took our place and bore our sins. He paid for them and purchased our redemption.

Third, we must repent of our sin. God has commanded men everywhere to repent. Acts 3:19 states, "Repent therefore and be converted, that your sins may be blotted out, so that times of refreshing may come from the presence of the Lord." What does this word *repent* mean? It means to change direction–to hang a U-turn on the road of life. It means to stop living the kind of life we led previously and start living the kind of life outlined in the pages of the Bible. Now we must change and be willing to make a break with the past.

Fourth, we must receive Jesus Christ into our hearts and lives. Being a Christian is having God Himself take residence in our lives. John 1:12 tells us, "But as many as received Him, to them He gave the right to become children of God." We must receive Him. Jesus said, "Behold, I stand at the door and knock. If anyone hears My voice and opens the door, I will come in…" (Revelation 3:20). Each one of us must individually decide to open the door. How do we open it? Through prayer.

If you have never asked Jesus Christ to come into your life, you can do it right now. Here is a suggested prayer you might even pray.

Lord Jesus, I know that I am a sinner and I am sorry for my sin. I turn and repent of my sins right now. Thank You for dying on the cross for me and paying the price for my sin. Please come into my heart and life right now. Fill me with Your Holy Spirit and help me to be Your disciple. Thank You for forgiving me and coming into my life. Thank You that I am now a child of Yours and that I am going to heaven. In Jesus' name, I pray. Amen.

When you pray that prayer God will respond. You have made the right decision–the decision that will impact how you spend eternity. Now you will go to heaven, and in the meantime, find peace and the answers to your spiritual questions.

Taken from: *Life. Any Questions?*
by Greg Laurie, Copyright © 1995. Used by permission.

Other books available in this series...

Spiritual Warfare
by Brian Brodersen
Pastor Brian Brodersen of Calvary Chapel Vista, California brings biblical balance and practical insight to the subject of spiritual warfare.

Christian Leadership
by Larry Taylor
Pastor Larry Taylor of the Calvary Chapel Bible College in Twin Peaks, California discusses the basics of leadership in the church and challenges us to become leaders that serve.

The Psychologizing of the Faith
by Bob Hoekstra
Pastor Bob Hoekstra of Living in Christ Ministries calls the church to leave the broken cisterns of human wisdom, and to return to the fountain of living water flowing from our wonderful counselor, Jesus Christ.

Practical Christian Living
by Wayne Taylor
Pastor Wayne Taylor of Calvary Fellowship in Seattle, Washington takes us through a study of Romans 12 and 13 showing us what practical Christian living is all about.

Building Godly Character
by Ray Bentley

Pastor Ray Bentley of Maranatha Chapel in San Diego, California takes us through a study in the life of David to show how God builds His character in our individual lives.

Worship and Music Ministry
by Rick Ryan & Dave Newton

Pastor Rick Ryan and Dave Newton of Calvary Chapel Santa Barbara, California give us solid biblical insight into the very important subjects of worship and ministering to the body of Christ through music.

Answers for the Skeptic
by Scott Richards

Pastor Scott Richards of Calvary Christian Fellowship of Tucson, Arizona gives us the basics in sharing our faith with the skeptic. He shows *what* to say when our faith is challenged, and *how* to answer.

Enjoying Bible Study
by Skip Heitzig

Pastor Skip Heitzig of Calvary Chapel Albuquerque, New Mexico shows us how to study the Bible, and *enjoy* it! Helpful tools for study and application are given to draw us into a deeper relationship with God.

Creation by Design
by Mark Eastman, M.D.

Mark Eastman, M.D., of Genesis Outreach in Temecula, California carefully examines and clarifies the evidence for a Creator God, and the depth of His relationship to mankind.

Effective Prayer Life
by Chuck Smith

Chuck Smith of Calvary Chapel Costa Mesa, California takes us through a study on the importance of having a fervent prayer life, and the results of such a life.

For ordering information, please write to The Word for Today, P.O. Box 8000, Costa Mesa, CA 92628, or call toll free (800) 272-WORD.